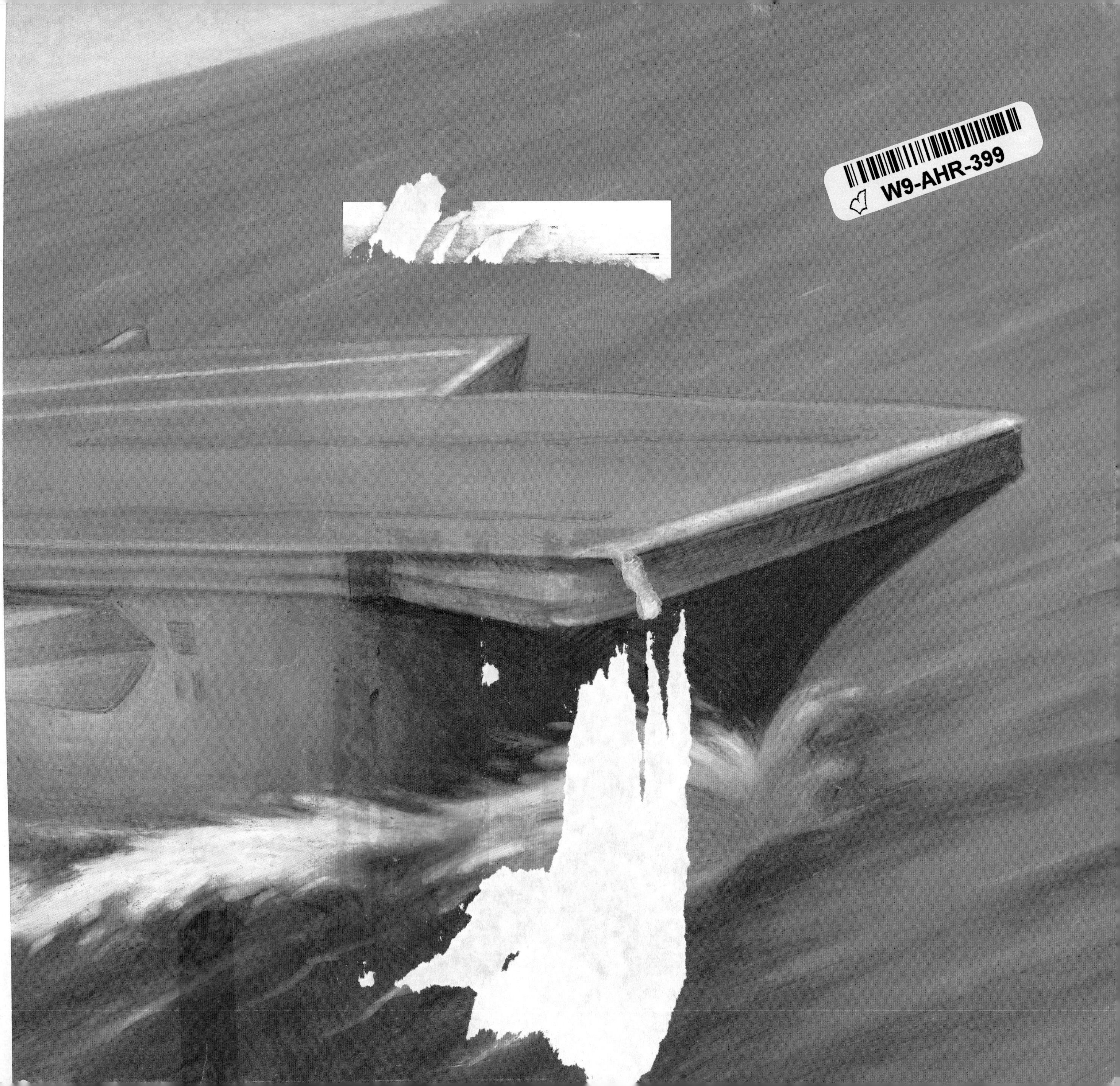

NUGGET ★
ON THE
FLIGHT DECK

Patricia Newman

illustrated by Aaron Zenz

Walker & Company   New York

Nugget:
a new aviator on his
first tour of duty

Mother:
a pilot's home ship

Welcome aboard, **Nugget**! I'm Lieutenant Jake Guttman, but you
can call me Gutts. I'll bet you've never been aboard a carrier before.
We call her **Mother** because she's our home, our own floating city,
with everything from a barbershop to a television station on board!
Let's check out my **bird** in the **hangar**.

Bird:
an aircraft; the bird in
this book is based on
the F/A-18F

Hangar:
a garage for aircraft,
which is three decks high

Hop:
a mission

Zero-dark-thirty:
after midnight but
before sunrise

Officer's mess:
the dining hall for
officers only

My first **hop** was at **zero-dark-thirty,** and I'm running on empty. Let's swing by the **officer's mess** for some **chow** on our way.

Stick with me, Nugget, so you don't get lost. Maps are posted at every **hatch** so new pilots like you can find their way around.

Watch your step on these steep stairs. We'll take a quick detour to my **rack**. Space is a real luxury on a carrier. But when I fly, I've got the whole world above and below me!

Chow:
food

Hatch:
a doorway on a ship

Rack:
a bunk bed stacked
four high on a ship

Welcome to the **basement**. There's my bird. Isn't she a beauty? She looks even better with her wings unfolded. Space is tight, even for aircraft!

First, put on a **zoombag**. Next, you'll need **speed jeans** to keep you from fainting when we're **pulling Gs** in a high climb or a nosedive. The survival vest goes on top. It has your life preserver and flares and radio in case we have to **punch out**. But don't worry. Safety's first with us pilots. I promise to bring you home in one piece.

Basement:
the main hangar deck
of the carrier

Zoombag:
a flight suit

Speed jeans:
a special suit that pilots wear
to keep from passing out
during high-G maneuvers

Pulling Gs:
one G is the force it takes to keep us on Earth—we call it gravity; while flying at high speed, fighter pilots may feel more than one G as a strong force pulling them back to Earth—and they can pull as many as twelve Gs (twelve times the force of normal gravity) in a steep climb or dive

Punch out:
to eject from an airplane

The Brown Shirt has got the **gouge** on our plane. He says it's in tip-top shape. Let's ride up in the elevator with it.

Watch out, Nugget! The Blue Shirt in the tractor is hurrying to haul our plane into position. Something happens every ten seconds up here on the **roof. Keep your head on a swivel** and you won't get hurt.

Our bird is almost ready. The Grapes fuel her, the Red Shirts load ammunition, and the White Shirts make sure everyone stays safe.

Gouge:
the latest
information

Roof:
the flight deck

**Keep your head
on a swivel**:
look around you
all the time

Okay, Nugget. Let's **kick the tires and light the fires!**
Strap yourself into the backseat. That Yellow Shirt is directing
us to the **waist cat**. He talks to us with his hands.

Kick the tires and light the fires: do the preflight check and take off quickly

Waist cat: one of the two catapults on the port, or left, side of the carrier; there are also two catapults at the bow, or front end, of the ship

You probably can't see him, but a Green Shirt is under our plane, hooking up the launch bar to the **catapult**. And look behind us. The **JBD** is about to go up. The Yellow Shirt gives us a thumbs-up on deck. Give him a salute, Nugget, and watch him pass control to the **shooter**.

Catapult:
a steam-powered device that "sling-shots" an aircraft off a carrier so it can build up enough speed for takeoff on the short 300-foot runway

JBD:
Jet Blast Deflector; a wall that is raised to protect the flight crew on deck from being blown off the ship by the aircraft's engines

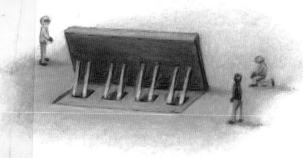

Shooter:
the catapult officer who gives the
signal to launch the aircraft

Cat stroke:
the path the
aircraft travels
after the catapult
releases it

Final ready:
the shooter's
signal to launch
the aircraft

Spooled up:
excited

We're going to full power. Feel the aircraft hunker down
as the catapult pulls us back? Just hold your breath down the
cat stroke. I'll do the rest. There's the **final ready**!

Yee-ha! Zero to two hundred miles per hour in three
seconds. We're **spooled up** now!

Our orders say to fly up to the **tanker** for some gas so we'll have enough for our practice **dogfight**. I'll radio the **island** to tell them what we're doing.
   "401 plugged and receiving."

Tanker:
an in-flight gas station; fighter planes use about 1,500 pounds of fuel every 15 minutes

Dogfight:
aerial combat, usually between two planes

Island:
the building on top of the flight deck from which officers direct all flight and ship operations

401 plugged and receiving:
radio talk for "plane number 401 is hooked up to the tanker and receiving fuel"

A dogfight is a test of wits, Nugget. Pilots need to make split-second decisions and our moves have to be perfect. And practice makes perfect, right? I've never lost a dogfight yet, and you're going to help me win now.

Bogey at **four o'clock**. He's really my pal Mookie, but he'll be our opponent today. We'll let him get a little closer . . . and then **break right**. He'll turn with us, but he's going so fast, he'll fly right by.

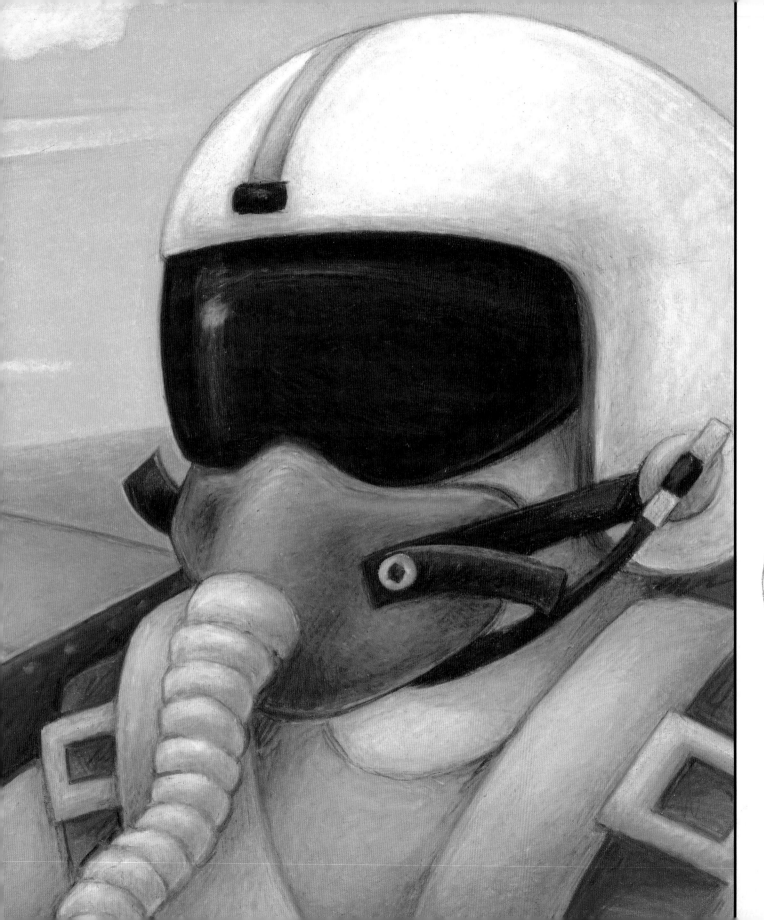

Bogey:
an unidentified
aircraft

Four o'clock:
the space around
a pilot is like a
clock: twelve
o'clock is straight
ahead; three
o'clock is directly
to the right; four
o'clock is to the
right and a little
behind the pilot

Break right:
make a hard
right turn

Scissors:
a diving, climbing, twisting maneuver in which
two planes weave back and forth; their paths
look like opposing Ss

Now we're on the attack. Mookie's giving us the old **scissors** move, trying to get behind us. **Check six** for me, Nugget! Watch this. We'll slow down and **pull up** hard into a **high yo-yo**. Hold on to your stomach! When Mookie flies by, we'll drop down behind him. He's in our sights now, and he knows it. Dogfight over! Give him a wave to thank him for the practice.

Check six:
look behind you;
six o'clock is to the
rear of the aircraft

Pull up:
pulling back on the
control stick to make
the plane fly higher

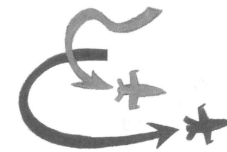

High yo-yo:
a move in which a pilot flies
high and then reduces speed
to drop behind a bogey

Bingo to Mom:
return to the aircraft
carrier with the
minimum amount
of fuel allowed

Buzzing the tower:
a supersonic flyby
of the tower or
island on the carrier

Time to **bingo to Mom**. We've got just enough fuel left.
How about **buzzing the tower** to celebrate our victory? Give 'em
the thumbs-up, Nugget. We're number one!

Hawk circle:
the circular path that pilots fly over the carrier when they're waiting to land

Three down and locked:
the three landing-gear wheels are lowered and locked into position, ready for landing

Port:
the left side of the ship

Let's slide into the **hawk circle** before landing. I've got
three down and locked.

Watch the lights for me on the **port** side of the ship. See
the yellow one? That's the **meatball**. If it's in the middle of
a row of green lights, we're good to go.

Meatball:
a yellow light that helps a pilot land on a carrier; the pilot is too high if the yellow
light is above the green lights, too low if the yellow light is below the green lights,
and on target for landing if the yellow light is in line with the green lights

When we touch down, we want our **tailhook** to grab an **arresting wire**. We need an **OK 3 wire** to make this a perfect mission, Nugget. Brace yourself. Landing feels mighty rough to a first-timer like you!

Tailhook:
an extended hook attached to the plane's tail used to catch one of the arresting wires in a carrier landing

Arresting wire:
one of four wires stretched across the stern, or back, of the carrier; aircraft tailhooks grab one of these wires, which can stop a 54,000–pound aircraft going 150 miles an hour in two seconds

OK 3 wire:
each landing is graded, and the highest grade is OK; the third arresting wire is the safest one to grab on a landing; pilots who consistently hook the third wire move up in the ranks

Bravo Zulu:
praise for a job
well done

Paddles:
the Landing Signal
Officer (LSO), who
helps pilots land
on deck and grades
their performance

Hear that **Bravo Zulu**, Nugget? That's for you!
Paddles gave us top marks for our landing.
From now on, you're Kid Bravo around here.

CARRIER FACTS

- Weight: about 12,000 school buses (60,000 tons or 54,430 metric tons)
- Size of flight deck: longer than 3 football fields (1,092 feet or 333 meters)
- Height: as tall as a 24-story building (244 feet or 74 meters)
- Weight of each anchor: about 5 male African elephants (30 tons or 27 metric tons)
- Weight of each link in the anchor chain: about 6 third graders (360 pounds or 163 kilograms)
- Number of meals served every day: 18,000 (for you, that's 3 meals a day for more than 16 years)
- Number of TVs on board: 3,000 (if you have 20 kids in your class, that's 150 TVs each)
- Number of dentists and doctors: 11
- Number of haircuts each week: 1,500 (for you, that's 1 haircut every day for more than 4 years)

A RAINBOW OF JOBS:

THE COLOR-CODED UNIFORMS OF THE CARRIER DECK CREW

Here's a short guide to the tasks handled by each team on the flight deck of
an aircraft carrier.

PURPLE	fuel planes; also called Grapes
BLUE	move planes to and from the hangar, scrub decks, put "chocks" around wheels to keep planes from rolling until they are ready to take off
GREEN	troubleshoot the catapult and arresting gear
YELLOW	give orders to Blue and Green Shirts to move planes around on deck
RED	handle crash, salvage, weapons, and explosives disposal
BROWN	maintain planes
WHITE	keep flight deck crew safe and healthy; White Shirts with a red cross assist when an airplane crashes

THE AVIATOR'S ALPHABET

Alpha	**H**otel	**O**scar	**V**ictor
Bravo	**I**ndia	**P**apa	**W**hiskey
Charlie	**J**uliet	**Q**uebec	**X**-Ray
Delta	**K**ilo	**R**omeo	**Y**ankee
Echo	**L**ima	**S**ierra	**Z**ulu
Foxtrot	**M**ike	**T**ango	
Golf	**N**ovember	**U**niform	

THE AUTHOR SALUTES

My father, a former marine awarded the Purple Heart, and men and women like him who defend and protect the United States; and my mother and spouses like her on the home front

This book would not have been possible without the support and patience of two expert pilots and longtime friends: Rear Admiral Dennis E. FitzPatrick, a United States Navy pilot (call sign Frailes) who commanded the Argonauts, an F/A-18 fighter squadron, and has landed aircraft on a carrier more than 655 times; and Dwan Wilson (call sign Mookie), a former United States Air Force captain and instructor pilot. Thanks also to the experts in my writing group—Erin Dealey, Connie Goldsmith, and Linda Joy Singleton—for their dedication to making me a better writer. Thanks to Deborah Warren for finding a home for this book, and to Emily Easton and the staff at Walker for their vision and enthusiasm.

THE ILLUSTRATOR SALUTES

Elijah, whom we first knew as "Nugget"

The artist wishes to thank Master Sergeant Jerry Lee Smith, Jr., MSGT USMC (ret) for his valuable input and for the wealth of knowledge he brought from his twenty-seven years of aircraft experience. For visual reference, the artist relied on the abundance of media generously provided by the United States Navy in the public gallery on their official Web site (www.navy.mil).

Text copyright © 2009 by Patricia Newman
Illustrations copyright © 2009 by Aaron Zenz

First published in the United States of America in 2009 by Walker Publishing Company, Inc.
Visit Walker & Company's Web site at www.walkeryoungreaders.com

For information about permission to reproduce selections from this book, write to
Permissions, Walker & Company, 175 Fifth Avenue, New York, New York 10010

Library of Congress Cataloging-in-Publication Data
Newman, Patricia.
Nugget on the flight deck / by Patricia Newman ; illustrated by Aaron Zenz.
            p.   cm.
Summary: Aboard an aircraft carrier, a lieutenant introduces a new aviator to the "lingo" and layout before taking him on a practice dogfight.
Includes bibliographical references.
ISBN-13: 978-0-8027-9735-3 • ISBN-10: 0-8027-9735-0 (hardcover)
ISBN-13: 978-0-8027-9736-0 • ISBN-10: 0-8027-9736-9 (reinforced)
[1. Naval art and science—Terminology—Fiction. 2. Aircraft carriers—Fiction. 3. Air pilots, Military—Fiction.] I. Zenz, Aaron, ill. II. Title.
PZ7.N4854Nug 2009   [E]—dc21   2008044673

Art created with Prismacolor colored pencils
Typeset in Campaign and Highlander
Book design by Danielle Delaney

Printed in China by SNP Leefung Printers Limited
2 4 6 8 10 9 7 5 3 1 (hardcover)
2 4 6 8 10 9 7 5 3 1 (reinforced)

All papers used by Walker & Company are natural, recyclable products made from wood grown in well-managed forests.
The manufacturing processes conform to the environmental regulations of the country of origin.

SOURCES

In addition to the sources listed below in the For Further Reading and Surfing section, the author also used the following source material for research.

Federation of American Scientists, Military Analysis Network. "US Navy Ships: Aircraft Carriers," http://www.fas.org/man/dod-101/sys/ship/cv.htm.

FitzPatrick, Dennis E. US Navy Rear Admiral (Lower Half) and former navy fighter pilot. 2003. Interview by the author via telephone. October 21.

Lightbody, Andy, and Joe Poyer. *The Complete Book of Top Gun: America's Flying Aces.* Lincolnwood, IL: Publications International, Ltd., 1990.

The Tailhook Association. "Aviator Slang." http://www.tailhook.org/AVSLANG.htm.

Wilson, Dwan. Commercial pilot and former US Air Force captain and pilot. 2003. Interview by the author in person. March 24 and March 26.

The illustrator relied upon the Navy's official Web site for photo reference and detail at http://www.navy.mil/view_photos_top.asp.

He was also fortunate to have the military expertise of Jerry Lee Smith, Jr., MSGT USMC (retired).

FOR FURTHER READING AND SURFING

Books
Beyer, Mark. *Aircraft Carriers Inside and Out.* New York: PowerPlus Books, 2002.

Dartford, Mark. *Fighter Planes.* Minneapolis: Lerner Publications Company, 2003.

Doyle, Kevin. *Aircraft Carriers.* Minneapolis: Lerner Publications Company, 2003.

Williams, Amy E., and Ted Williams, ill. *The American Fighter Plane.* New York: MetroBooks, 2002.

DVD/Video
Carrier. DVD, directed by Maro Chermayeff. Santa Monica, CA: Icon Productions, 2008. 600 minutes.

The Big Aircraft Carrier. VHS, directed by William VanDerKloot. Atlanta, GA: Little Mammoth Media, a division of VanDerKloot Film & Television, 1995. 40 minutes.

Web Sites
Harris, Tom. "How Aircraft Carriers Work." http://www.howstuffworks.com/aircraft-carrier.htm.

"Carrier: Life Aboard the Aircraft Carrier *USS Nimitz*." http://www.pbs.org/weta/carrier.

"The Aircraft Carrier." http://www.navy.mil/navydata/ships/carriers/carriers.asp.